JUN '03

MW01006742

811.54   Piercy, Marge.
PIERCY
          Colors passing
          through us.

$23.00

DATE			

Colors Passing Through Us

Colors Passing Through Us

P O E M S   B Y

MARGE PIERCY

Alfred A. Knopf   New York   2003

THIS IS A BORZOI BOOK
PUBLISHED BY ALFRED A. KNOPF

Copyright © 2003 by Middlemarsh, Inc.

www.randomhouse.com/knopf/poetry

Knopf, Borzoi Books and the colophon are registered
trademarks of Random House, Inc.

Acknowledgments of previous publication of the poems
may be found following the last poem.

Library of Congress Cataloging-in-Publication Data
Piercy, Marge.
Colors passing through us : poems / by Marge Piercy. — 1st ed.
      p.   cm.
ISBN 0-375-41537-8
I. Title.
PS3566.I4 C65   2003
811'.54—dc21   2002066145

Manufactured in the United States of America
First Edition

Contents

WOMEN OF DARK HOUSES

OTHERWISE

WINTER PROMISES

LITTLE LIGHTS

COLORS PASSING THROUGH US

RISING IN PERILOUS HOPE

Women of Dark Houses

Photograph of my mother sitting on the steps

My mother who isn't anyone's
just her own intact and yearning
self complete as a birch tree
sits on the tenement steps.

She is awkwardly lovely, her face
pure as a single trill perfectly
prolonged on a violin, yet she
knows the camera sees her

and she arranges her body
like a flower in a vase to be
displayed, admired she hopes.
She longs to be luminous

and visible, to shine in the eyes
of it must be a handsome man,
who will carry her away—and he
will into poverty and an abortion

but not yet. Now she drapes
her best, her only good dress
inherited from her sister who dances
on the stage, around her legs

that she does not like
and leans a little forward

because she does like her breasts.
How she wants love to bathe

her in honeyed light lifting her
up through smoky clouds clamped
on the Pittsburgh slum. Blessed
are we who cannot know

what will come to us,
our upturned faces following
through the sky
the sun of love.

In the attic of dreams

I imagine an attic
huge and dusty and crowded with old trunks.
In it, I dig and winnow
I sort and scavenge.

Old diaries emerge—
my unknown great grandmothers'—
their secrets and troubles,
their visions and terrors

rise from moth-chewed clothes
stowed away, huge bright io
moths themselves, all the yellowed
pages still legible in tiny letters.

Their cries and laughter have
long since sunk into the bloody earth,
stirred into the ocean salt
of the sea their children crossed.

I dream I am walking through
a field of their voices like ripe
wheat and the wind whistles
into my ears their stories and songs.

One reason I like opera

In movies, you can tell the heroine
because she is blonder and thinner
than her sidekick. The villainess
is darkest. If a woman is fat,
she is a joke and will probably die.

In movies, the blondest are the best
and in bleaching lies not only purity
but victory. If two people are both
extra pretty, they will end up
in the final clinch.

Only the flawless in face and body
win. That is why I treat
movies as less interesting
than comic books. The camera
is stupid. It sucks surfaces.

Let's go to the opera instead.
The heroine is fifty and weighs
as much as a '65 Chevy with fins.
She could crack your jaw in her fist.
She can hit high C lying down.

The tenor the women scream for
wolfs down an eight course meal daily.
He resembles a bull on hind legs.
His thighs are the size of beer kegs.
His chest is a redwood with hair.

Their voices twine, golden serpents.
Their voices rise like the best
fireworks and hang and hang
then drift slowly down descending
in brilliant and still fiery sparks.

The hippopotamus baritone (the villain)
has a voice that could give you
an orgasm right in your seat.
His voice smokes with passion.
He is hot as lava. He erupts nightly.

The contralto is, however, svelte.
She is supposed to be the soprano's
mother, but is ten years younger,
beautiful and Black. Nobody cares.
She sings you into her womb where you rock.

What you see is work like digging a ditch,
hard physical labor. What you hear
is magic as tricky as knife throwing.
What you see is strength like any
great athlete's. What you hear

is still rendered precisely as the best
Swiss watchmaker. The body is
resonance. The body is the cello case.
The body just is. The voice loud
as hunger remagnetizes your bones.

The good old days at home sweet home

On Monday my mother washed.
It was the way of the world,
all those lines of sheets flapping
in the narrow yards of the neighborhood,
the pulleys stretching out second
and third floor windows.

Down in the dank steamy basement,
wash tubs vast and grey, the wringer
sliding between the washer
and each tub. At least every
year she or I caught
a hand in it.

Tuesday my mother ironed.
One iron was the mangle.
She sat at it feeding in towels,
sheets, pillow cases.
The hand ironing began
with my father's underwear.

She ironed his shorts.
She ironed his socks.
She ironed his undershirts.
Then came the shirts,
a half hour to each, the starch
boiling on the stove.

I forgot bluing. I forgot
the props that held up the line
clattering down. I forgot
chasing the pigeons that shat
on her billowing housedresses.
I forgot clothespins in the teeth.

Tuesday my mother ironed my
father's underwear. Wednesday
she mended, darned socks on
a wooden egg. Shined shoes.
Thursday she scrubbed floors.
Put down newspapers to keep

them clean. Friday she
vacuumed, dusted, polished,
scraped, waxed, pummeled.
How did you become a feminist
interviewers always ask,
as if to say, when did this

rare virus attack your brain?
It could have been Sunday
when she washed the windows,
Thursday when she burned

the trash, bought groceries
hauling the heavy bags home.

It could have been any day
she did again and again what
time and dust obliterated
at once until stroke broke
her open. I think it was Tuesday
when she ironed my father's shorts.

Her body inscribes

for a ballet dancer who died of anorexia

Her body inscribes an arc like a fine metal
point, her body is a feather floating.
Her bones are those of a swallow,
her bones are chalky.
Her bones are hollow as flutes.

Her flesh is only lacquer on muscles
taut and overworked, tendons
that ping like breaking violin strings,
joints forced the wrong way,
blood in her toe shoes.

Even though she has no flesh
still she bleeds from her feet.
She is a perfect dream of light
bent to earth in her feathered tutu,
face remote, smile brilliant

over the dying body as a lamp
illuminating a vision of fleshless
grace, an angel of bones gleaming,
pain as an art form patronized
by eaters of large expensive dinners.

Lost

Women of dark houses
houses of ash,
houses of papier mâché
houses built of tomb
stones and granite memory,
your voices twist
tornadoes of dust.

Your dreams float
on the night pale
streamers dissolving
in moonlight
like thin wafers.
You weep milk.
It rises.

I have seen you
passing the windows
of old houses
after the summer people
have gone like warblers
south—to the warm
city flickering.

I have seen you
on the back road
on moonless nights
looking for something
lost, dropped,

stolen. Headlights
stab you away.

Women of lost names,
pollen on the wind,
history forgets you.
All that remain
are houses like dark
lanterns enclosing
dim fiery pain.

The glamour of it

The glamour of it to a child all sniffing
sniffling nose, with as many fingers
as a caterpillar has legs, to feel
the silken dresses, the plush
bathrobe, the velvet jacket
that no longer buttoned over her.

The drawers were even lusher:
scraps of old evening dresses,
brown lace over green slip,
bits of beading, an evening
purse that, shhh! she wore
with my brother's father, not mine.

It was slithery metal with scales
like a silver snake. A tortoise
shell comb bobeh had worn.
My mother's hair was always
shorn. Grandma's shimmered
down her back as she unpinned.

As we loosed these battered
treasures from their drawer,
faint old perfume shook out
of them. And Mother whispered
stories, shhh! her youth.
Memories thick as black velvet

leaked knowledge, its spicy
scent, into my ears. I learned
early my parents were human
too. I breathed in scandals, secrets,
the tang of dead lies. My
curiosity fattened on those scraps.

My mother gives me her recipe

Take some flour. Oh, I don't know,
like two-three cups, and you cut
in the butter. Now some women
they make it with shortening,
but I say butter, even though
that means you had to have fish, see?

You cut up some apples. Not those
stupid sweet ones. Apples for the cake,
they have to have some bite, you know?
A little sour in the sweet, like love.
You slice them into little moons.
No, no! Like half or crescent
moons. You aren't listening.

You mix sugar and cinnamon and cloves,
some women use allspice, till it's dark
and you stir in the apples. You coat
every little moon. Did I say you add
milk? Oh, just till it feels right.
Use your hands. Milk in the cake part!

Then you pat it into a pan, I like
round ones, but who cares?
I forgot to say you add baking powder.
Did I forget a little lemon on the apples?
Then you just bake it. Well, till it's done
of course. Did I remember you place
the apples in rows? You can make

16

a pattern, like a weave. It's pretty
that way. I like things pretty.

It's just a simple cake.
Any fool can make it
except your aunt. I
gave her the recipe
but she never
got it right.

The day my mother died

I seldom have premonitions of death.
That day opened like any
ordinary can of tomatoes.

The alarm drilled into my ear.
The cats stirred and one leapt off.
The scent of coffee slipped into my head

like a lover into my arms and I sighed,
drew the curtains and examined
the face of the day.

I remember no dreams of loss.
No dark angel rustled ominous wings
or whispered gravely.

I was caught by surprise
like the trout that takes the fly
and I gasped in the fatal air.

You were gone suddenly as a sound
fading in the coil of the ear
no trace, no print, no ash

just the emptiness of stilled air.
My hunger feeds on itself.
My hands are stretched out

to grasp and find only their
own weight bearing them down
toward the dark cold earth.

Too long dead

I just came on it like a rake in the grass
rising to deliver a sharp knock.
You have been dead sixteen years.
Too long. Too long. Can I remember?

You could come back as a cat
in a shelter and I would come save
you from execution, take you home,
spoil you with treats and caresses.

You could come back as a peony.
The ants live there, you said, no harm
done. Peonies outlive humans. The first
brought from China still bloom.

You could appear as a heron stalking
in the marsh using your old anger
as a spear to impale the fish
and you would lose your hunger.

You came the other night in a dream.
I was petting my cat Arofa who died
before you, and you were at the stove
putting a sour cherry pie in the oven.

I love cinnamon, it's so warm, you
said. *Always use lots of cinnamon.*
You make my apple cake but not
sweet enough, never sweet enough.

Suddenly I said, "But you're both dead.
I can't touch you." *But you can,* you
said smiling the way you did the rare
times when someone gave you a present.

You said to me, *As long as you live.*
Arofa said, *Now we have become you.*
And then very slowly you both vanished
in a gust of cherries and cinnamon.

Long night of the incomplete

In the brief light of the solstice
the wall of ice presses in, inex-
orable glacier, glinting cliffs
casting long blue shadows.

The birds are avid at the feeders.
The squirrels jostle them.
A coyote lurked at the foot
of the drive last night, then

turned smoke. I try to coax
the cats in before dusk
threatens. Wind whooshes
in the chimney. Flesh

does not flourish in such cold.
The death of my mother:
a tooth extracted years ago
yet the tongue still probes.

We fence, we fight, we pry,
we protect armored like goalies,
we lie, we promise, we fudge,
we are bribed and coerced.

Then one night it stops—
the worn out clock of the heart.
A silence parched and rusty,
a silence hollow and gnarled,

metallic, rasps on the mind.
The words never spoken,
unasked questions rattle,
beads of a broken necklace.

It does not come to an end,
this long night of regrets,
this unfinished conversation
dying in the throat like the year.

Jolly woman with birds

Poor woman, my mother said of Ada,
her friend, for she had no children.
A child, I could not comprehend
the tones of pity and condescension,
taffy dipped in vinegar and well salted.

Ada had canaries. In those days,
they were fed hempseed, got high
and sang their little yellow asses off.
Her house was filled with twittering
and song, and occasionally

an egg was laid and hatched.
Her house felt like a meadow
of goldenrod that sang in interlaced
melodies, as if a secret sun
shone under Detroit's lead ceiling

only for Ada. I loved to sit
at the table in her breakfast
nook, an exotic phrase that sweetened
my tongue like her hard candy
with soft centers. Nook, nook:

that was something a large bird
might cry from a rocky crag.
Ada's cakes were many layered
full of surprises—cherry jam,
big fat raisins, tiny currants,

chocolate chips. I thought I
would not mind being Ada (I
knew I would not be my mother)
savoring strawberry lemon cake
surrounded by the passion of birds.

Still the desert

for Joy Harjo

Daughter of the desert
turning like earth itself between
the red sun and the black moon
can you find what you need
beneath the tangled skein of freeways?

It is all desert still, although
the city fathers have sucked water
from the mountains to pretend
this is a huge oasis
with dry rivers of cement.

Will the right dates of beginning
and ending fall from the palms
into your palm? Will the night
winds whisper the syllables
of your secret name of power?

You will sit on the continent's back door
step and let the restless waters
carry to your feet a message
not in a bottle but in a poisoned
fish whose scales shine in the dark.

Words and music, music and words
gyre from you on the night where cars
swarm like locusts and oil wells
in yards pump their hearts' blood.
Your blood runs underground here.

Your sacred beauty is dangerous.
You bring fire into a tent of plastic wrap.
Words are helium. You could ignite
them or yourself: a poet kneeling
on a dump of used and wasted images.

In the department store

The women who work at cosmetics
counters terrify me. They seem molded
of superior plastic or light metal.
They could be shot up into orbit
never mussing a hair, make-up intact.

When I walk through, they never pester
me, never attack me with loud perfume,
never wheedle me into a make-over.
Perhaps I scare them too, leaking
some subversive pheromone.

I trot through like a raccoon
in an airport. They see me,
they look and turn away. Perhaps
I am a project they fear to tackle
too wild, too wooly, trailing

electrical impulses from my loose
black hair. They fasten on the throat
of the neat fortyish blond behind me
like stoats, dragging her to their
padded stools. A lost cause,

I sidle past into men's sporting
gear, safe but bemused, wondering
if they judge me too far gone
to salvage or smell my stubborn
unwillingness like rank musk.

Love has certain limited powers

The dead walk with us briefly,
suddenly just behind on the narrow
path like a part in the hairy grass.
We feel them between our shoulder
blades and we can speak, but if
we turn, like Eurydice they're gone.

The dead lie with us briefly
swimming through the warm salty
pool of darkness flat as flounders,
floating like feathers on the shafts
of silver moonlight. Their hair
brushes our face and is gone.

The dead speak to us through
the scent of red musk roses,
through steam rising from green tea,
through the spring rain scratching
on the pane. If I try to recapture
your voice, silence grates

in my ears, the mocking rush
of silence. But months later
I stand at the stove stirring a pot
of soup and you say, *Too much salt,*
and you say, *You have my hair,*
and, *Pain wears out like anything else.*

After the darkness

Her laughter caught like smoke
in her throat, her laugh
half velvet and half cough.

Her hair hummed with electric
sparks, always rising
to the hand and the comb, crackling.

Her hands toward the end looked
as if they had been underwater
too long, swollen, worn smooth.

They seemed to leave no prints.
The sparks in her eyes dimmed.
Her narrow shoulders drew together

to avoid a blow. "He sits in his chair
and watches me while I sweep,"
she said, "as if I haven't been cleaning

for sixty years." When the lightning
stroke charred her brain, she turned
to it, a clean bed freshly made.

She turned into the darkness,
leaving her laughter, her skin,
her hair, her heart slowing

like a muted drum. She touched
my mind once sharply, a shock,
then like smoke she blew away.

What's left? A jade necklace,
the ring cut from her dead finger,
her laugh that breaks in my throat.

Chrysanthemum season

It comes round again, round
again, chrysanthemum season, rust
and golden with their acrid scent
colors of leaves falling on your grave.

I never felt you there, not even
when we tossed the dirt in handfuls
when the rabbi who did not know
you hunched like a raven over your

wasted body wrapped in white.
I never felt you a year later
when the simple stone was placed
over you. To me you were made

of warm slack lap, chestnut hair
long as Rapunzel's streaked grey
as if paint had run: and words,
Yiddish, Russian, busted English

slewed sideways in your soft
mouth that so often kissed me.
You fed me stories with your
soup and I grew up into them.

My dreams, Hannah, are built
of your stories. They dye my brain
purple and golden, black
and red and the grey of terror.

Hunting the hunter

Every woman has chased Orion
up the greasy slope of midnight,
his leather smelling of sweat,
of gunpowder, of something dead
and spicy a dog might roll in.

Every woman has leaned into that
embrace as cold as a bullet
as hot as a bullet,
his swift and lethal laugh
his hands of cobalt and lead.

Every woman has impaled herself
as a shrike keeps dragonflies
and small birds on thorns
in his larder, has mistaken
poison spines for blossoms.

He is the hunter who hilts
fire at his belt, who loves
not you but the great bear he
chases all winter, in whose
arms his bones will snap.

Your scent burns off him
like a cloud off a granite ledge.
You are the hunter now.
What you chase is your shadow
cast by the rising moon.

The clock in the closet

I'll never get old, says the fifteen-year-old,
knowing that when they ask her,
she'll just say no. No thank you.
I'll stay eighteen, I'll stop at twenty-
eight or thirty-five or forty-two.
Only a moron or a masochist would
accept more years, like a dish
of overcooked fish passed you
at a dinner party. Just refuse.

There is choice if you have the money:
go under the scalpel once, twice,
seven times. Liposuction, face
lifts, eye jobs, botulin inserted under
the skin, a peel or two. You don't
exactly look young, but you
have seized power over your body:
made yourself into an artifact
like a tight and pretty death mask.

Every aging woman knows that inside,
behind her face, her scrawny neck
and puffy cheeks, the same swan
girl swims over her reflection:
we are all that we once were
behind the mirror in that downy cave.
The same gaze measures the world.
If the ghost did rise from the failing
body, what age would it be?

Myself, I can't spare a single year.
I see my younger selves on landings
of that winding stair of years, gesticulating,
weeping, banging my head on the stone
of indifference, clawing until my hands
bled on the granite flesh of cold lovers,
fighting the wrong battles in the right wars,
dropping words that would swarm me, stinging.
I wring what wisdom I own from every hour.

Otherwise

No one came home

1.
Max was in bed that morning, pressed
against my feet, walking to my pillow
to kiss my nose, long and lean with aqua-
marine eyes, my sun prince who thought

himself my lover. He was cream and golden
orange, strong willed, lord of the other
cats and his domain. He lay on my chest
staring into my eyes. He went out at noon.

He never came back. A smear of blood
on the grass at the side of the road
where we saw a huge coyote the next
evening. We knew he had been eaten

yet we could not know. We kept looking
for him, calling him, searching. He
vanished from our lives in an hour. My cats
have always died in old age, slowly

with abundant warning. Not Max.
He left a hole in my waking.

2.
A woman leaves her children in day care,
goes off to her secretarial job
on the 100th floor, conscientious always
to arrive early, because she needs the money

for her children, for health insurance,
for rent and food and clothing and fees
for all the things kids need, whose father
has two new children and a great lawyer.

They are going to eat chicken that night
she has promised, and the kids talk of that
together, fried chicken with adobo, rice
and black beans, food rich as her love.

The day is bright as a clean mirror.

3.
His wife has morning sickness so does
not rise for breakfast. He stops for coffee,
a yogurt, rushing for the 8:08 train.
Ignoring the window, he writes his five

pages, the novel that is going to make
him famous, cut him loose from the desk
where he is chained to the phone
eight to ten hours, making cold calls.

In his head, naval battles rage. He
has been studying Midway, the Coral
Sea, Guadalcanal. He can recite
tonnage, tides, the problems with torpedoes.

For five years, he has prepared.
His makeshift office in the basement
is lined with books and maps. His book
will sing with bravery and error.

The day is blue and whistles like a robin.

4.
His father was a fireman and his brother.
He once imagined being a rock star
but by the end of high school, he knew
it was his calling, it was his family way.

As there are trapeze families, clans
who perform with tigers or horses,
the Irish travelers, tinkers, gypsies,
those born to work the earth of their farm,

and those who inherit vast fortunes
built of the bones of others, so families
inherit danger and grace, the pursuit
of the safety of others before their own.

The morning smelled of the river,
of doughnuts, of coffee, of leaves.

5.
When a man fell into the molten steel
the company would deliver an ingot
to bury. Something. Where I live

on the Cape, lost at sea means no body.

You can't bury a coffin length of sea
water. There are stones in our grave
yards with lists of names, the sailors
from the ships gone down in a storm.

MIA means no body, no answer,
hope that is hopeless, the door
that can never be quite closed.
Lives are broken off like tree limbs

in a storm. Other lives simply dissolve
like salt in warm water and there is
no shadow on the pavement, no trace.
They puff into nothing. We can't believe.

We die still expecting an answer.

6.
Los desaparecidos. Did we notice?
Did we care? In Chile, funded,
assisted by the CIA, a democratic
government was torn down and thousands

brought into a stadium and never seen
again. Reports of torture, reports of graves
in the mountains, bodies dumped at sea,
reports of your wife, your son, your

father arrested and then vanished
like cigarette smoke, gone like
a whisper you aren't quite sure you
heard, a living person who must, who

must be somewhere, anywhere, lost,
wounded, boxed in a cell, in exile,
under a stone, somewhere, bones,
a skull, a button, a wisp of cloth.

In Argentina, the women marched
for those who had disappeared.
Did we notice? That happened
in those places, those other places

where people didn't speak English,
ate strange spicy foods, had dictators
or Communists or sambas or goas.
They didn't count. We didn't count

them or those they said had been
there alive and now who knew?
Not us. The terror has come home.
Will it make us better or worse?

7.
When will we understand what terrorists
never believe, that we are all

precious in our loving, all tender
in our flesh and webbed together?

That no one should be torn
out of the fabric of friends and family,
the sweet and sour work of loving,
burnt anonymously, carelessly

because of nothing they ever did
because of hatred they never knew
because of nobody they ever touched
or left untouched, turned suddenly

to dust on a perfect September
morning bright as a new apple
when nothing they did would
ever again make any difference.

The true patriot

I am Efran, says she.
There are only two hundred of us.
We are engaged in a bloody civil war.

I was in the Ukraine purchasing nuclear
weapons to annihilate the enemy.
They are petitioning the World Court

and the UN to intervene.
We live by eating each other's hearts.
Last week we were three hundred.

There can be no compromise with the
sons of pigs. I am composing
the National Epic of my side.

By next week no one will survive
who can read it, but it will live
on in the memories of our unborn

ancestors. Nationalism is all.
Only Efra forever, long after
there are none of us left.

Dirty old century: 12-31-99

It's about time for a change of centuries.
This one is getting stale fast.

It's a cheat who has lied too many times
to believe anything it says, even goodbye.

Progress, it came in bellowing,
machinery will set you free and bring

abundance to everyone. No one
will be hungry, no one will die

of thirst. Flies will no longer feast
on the eyes of brown babies.

Then came the war to end all wars,
then the bigger war after that.

By century's end, no one will be sick
any longer, robots will clean our houses,

we will fly to the moon for pleasure.
Who ever heard of pollution?

We will become more and more rational,
more civilized. How's your horoscope today?

Michael Jackson gives birth to Martian;
Elvis has appeared as the Madonna

on a bank window in Texas. This century
is a mansion built on the Grand Boulevard

in 1900, all the newest conveniences,
lots of rooms for the servants. Now

it's a whorehouse upstairs and downstairs
a faith healer blesses the cancer patients.

In the garage the brightest kid on the block
is cooking crystal meth. The toilets

have backed up. The yard is full of old tires
and paint cans and tampon injectors.

We, your parents and grandparents
and great grandparents pass on to you

one used century for your enjoyment.
Or you could build something else.

Got the 21st century blues

Woke up this morning,
bed like a slab of cement.
Breath, steam on frosty air.
Furnace asleep and won't stir.
I'm gonna go live in a yurt.

Waiting for the furnace man to come.

Turned on my computer.
Windows crashed Dragon.
Email is out all day.
I lost my voice recognition file.
I want a wigwam, feathers in my hair.

Waiting for the furnace man to come.
Waiting for Microsoft to answer.

Spent the day waiting
for the cable guy.
After he left at five thirty
no sound on 240 channels.
I'm retiring to a Trappist monastery.

Waiting for the furnace man to come.
Waiting for Microsoft to answer.
Waiting for the cable company to call back.

Machines call me up
to sell me Florida condos.
The propane is leaking

again from the tank.
I want to move into a cave and wrestle bears.

Waiting for the furnace man to come.
Waiting for Microsoft to answer.
Waiting for the cable company to call back.
Waiting for the propane truck to arrive.

I am glad all these gadgets
have made my life
so fucking convenient
I never can relax any more.
Maybe a hole in a hollow tree.

I have 240 channels and no sound.
I have 120 gigabytes and no files.
I have a furnace and stove
cold as marble slabs
as I wait for the furnace man,

Microsoft, the cable company,
wait for the propane man
wait for the revolution
wait for the messiah. Wait
for a nice deep hole in the frozen ground.

Resort offseason

It is snowing on the mainland.
Out here drops are spaced
like globelights along black
branches, and the slow rain

eases down. On Nantucket
when the year-rounders plan
to fly to the mainland, they say,
"I'm going to America."

We're not that wooly.
Still we are connected by two
only bridges where traffic
can back up for ten miles.

The summer people are other.
We live off them, not very
well. Our real life is with
each other, feuds snarly

for two generations, friends
who really come when you call.
We barter. We gossip
in the middle of the street

truck window to truck
window while tourists honk
and stew. Red foxes,
muskrats, coyotes, possums,

and us, a little wilder
than you might think
living on and off
this fragile bar of sand.

Minor losses

On the way to a farm in Maine
we used to stop for ice cream
rich as roses, thick as blackberry brambles,
butter and honey and summer itself.
On the walls: photos of prize bulls,
cows victorious at the state fair.
Behind glass, husband or wife churned
in fifteen flavors, the floor humming.
Outside, a field where companionable
cows watched you drive up,
switching their tails in August heat.

The last time we stopped,
thin ice cream brittle with ice crystals
chemical flavor. No cows. Tract
houses going up where hay had rippled.
The machinery is still. As we watched
a van pulled up with supermarket vats.
Out front a sign still says, home made.
A minor loss. So do the real things
pass from our lives like cows
grazing with heavy pink udders
where tract houses now sprout.

The disintegration

We watch the marriage of friends
wear through like a once warm
woolen sock through which suddenly
the thickened big toenail peers.

There is a tone in which couples
address each other that strips
veneer from the furniture,
that curdles milk and turns wine

to vinegar. He drowns out
her tentative pleading voice; she
whispers on the phone secrets
of his failures like poison pellets.

He jokes about her weight.
She weeps into his soup.
Their bed grows wide as a mountain
valley down which a glacier crawls.

Leaving is not the worst thing
husbands do; divorce doesn't
end life the way contempt freezes
it like marrow drying in the bones.

We can only watch, spectators
at a slow disaster, not a wreck

but a gradual poisoning of a field
that once bore healthy crops.

Now all we can hope is that the house
at last falls down, the creep of misery
fades into grieving, with the dying
finally pronounced entirely dead.

Finest porcelain

We gaze at the perfect gleaming
covered bowls of fine porcelain
painted with willows bowing
into calm water, with boats drifting
in casual elegance down a calm
stream where laughter floats
like confetti unknown to gravity.

The colors are clear, harmonious.
We smell lemon verbena and rose
petals. The taste would be of fine
green tea, perhaps jasmine.
We can add a little lemon
for contrast. Should we envy
or enjoy the scenery of those lives?

That life splits from top to bottom
like a worn out silk dress.
That life cracks open
and spills its bloody yolk.
That life opens like the beak
of a wounded gull and screams
raising hair on the back of my arms.

Porcelain is ground into the carpet.
Tea stains the pattern of ferns.
We made you up, your harmony,
your exquisite balance. The glitter
we saw was not faceted diamonds
but salt drying on a bruised cheek.

Family values

The man next door worked the line at Fords.
A tall man, he looked a bit sun dried
like a prune in spite of his bulk and pallor
and the red scar on his arm from the line.

Fridays after he got paid he went to one
of those bars that line up near the factories
to get a first shot at the check, where they will
cash them for no fee, and why not?

He never got home on payday until ten
or sometimes midnight. We always
knew because that soft voice of his
usually stuck in his throat like cotton batting

would rise, an electric saw caught in a board.
I would hear the curses hanging
like shooting stars in the bedroom's dark
and I would try to judge them for liveliness

originality and merit, for by the time
I was seven, I appreciated a good curse.
My mother was better, frankly, with Yiddish
as backup when English failed, but he was

persistent and wounded, leaking pity
like battery acid from every pore. If we
drifted to sleep, we would soon wake
because he would begin beating his kids,

the little ones first, and throwing them
out the grade door to crash against
the flimsy asbestos shingled wall of our
house. He worked his way through the boys

and the girl, with his wife slamming
out the door last. Then he would lock
the door and go to sleep, and we would
hear them sobbing, cursing, milling

in the driveway. No one ever spoke
of it. No one called the police and besides
didn't he have a right? He was the father.
He brought home what was left of his paycheck.

They were like a dozen other families
on the street, no worse. The father who beat
his daughter naked with his belt; the mother
who withheld food to punish till her son

would go garbage picking for his hunger,
the cop whose wife lay in a darkened room
with bruises on her face. Families were strong
then, yes, strong as gulags

strong as the iron maiden embracing you
with her spikes, strong as cyanide

but killing you far more slowly. I can
hear still the bodies hitting the siding

under my window till the glass rattled
and their sobs on the close indifferent night.

Gifts that keep on giving

You know when you unwrap them:
fruitcake is notorious. There were only
fifty-one of them baked in 1916 by the
personal chef of Rasputin. The mad monk
ate one. That was what finally killed him.

But there are many more bouncers:
bowls green and purple spotted like lepers.
Vases of inept majolica in the shape
of wheezing frogs or overweight lilies.
Sweaters sized for Notre-Dame's hunchback.

Hourglasses of no use humans
can devise. Gloves to fit three-toed sloths.
Mufflers of screaming plaid acrylic.
Necklaces and pins that transform
any outfit to a thrift shop reject.

Boxes of candy so stale and sticky
the bonbons pull teeth faster than
your dentist. Weird sauces bought
at warehouse sales no one will ever
taste unless suicidal or blind.

Immortal as vampires, these gifts
circulate from birthdays to Christmas,

from weddings to anniversaries.
Even if you send them to the dump,
they resurface, bobbing up on the third

day like the corpses they call floaters.
After all living have turned to dust
and ashes, in the ruins of cities
alien archeologists will judge our
civilization by these monstrous relics.

Kamasutra for dummies

Years ago I had a lover who got bored.
He liked a challenge. I was
too easily pleased to fluff his ego.
He bought a manual. We would
work our way through the positions.

Work is the operant word. I remember
his horny toenails and ripe feet
either side of my eyes and cheeks.
I remember arching my back
like a cat, the ache just looming.

In some positions his prick slipped
out every other stroke and he would
curse. It was sensual as those videos
to flatten your abs or firm your buttocks
where three young women whose abs

are flat as floorboards grin like rigor
mortis as they demonstrate some
overpriced 800 number device.
They never sweat. But we did.
We used chairs. And tables and stools.

Always the manual was open beside us
guiding our calisthenics. Spontaneous

as a presidential speech, exciting
as a lecture on actuarial tables
he staked my quivering libido through

its smoking heart. The night he wanted
to try it standing with me upsidedown
I left him hanging from the door
and whoosh, zoomed off like a rabid bat
to find someone who actually liked sex.

He left but can't let go

The old house wraps its cold around
you and slips into your veins
a lethal injection, whispering

you murderer. You turn away
you run from this place at dawn
your pockets full of anger

rattling like marbles, muttering.
You slip back every few years
to some holiday gathering

like an arsonist returning to stare
at his fire and then you slide out
again taking nothing, leaving

a few sharp words like nails
in the carpeting they would step on
days later and bleed, surprised.

Now they are gone who gave you
life and tried to smother it,
gone into the cold slithering

up your arm. You open your mouth
to speak and the words die. Who
now will monitor your ruin?

Not in the dark

The gold toothed wheel churns
up the blue road, the golden wheel
spiked and burning.

I saw death dancing in a rain
of bright feathers, standing
on the chest of my friend.

The breath rattled like a snake.
The heart was laboring.
I don't want to die in the darkness

he said. And now he asks
in the brazen hot morning
Is it getting light?

It lightens and he darkens
into burnt feathers, ashes
that choke him, darkness

welling up from within
like water rising quickly
gushing to the surface

then subsiding
into a dreadful burning
silence. Wet ashes.

How it was with us, dear grandchildren

Visions hounded us like angry wasps
stinging our eyelids heavy,
so we wept blood and stones.

Yet light rose in us at once pure
and molten, light the color of raw
honey, light the color of lava

spilling from the crater, igniting
the mountain to instant flame.
We burned our days

and our nights smouldered.
Much of it turned to ashes
in our mouths, clinkers

in our beds. Dead lava
like asphalt smothering the earth
with all its tender shoots buried.

Yet soon the insects return
buzzing and flitting. The first
wild grasses poke their green

spears through the cracks.
Strange deep purple and golden

wildflowers open their lush

velvet petals. One morning
a new and less apocalyptic vision
will rise like a minor sun, giving

warmth instead of fire. We'll get
up and walk out into its light
following a path new and familiar

at once, up on the mountain again
through canyons, seeing that the way
is long and we never ourselves will arrive.

Winter Promises

Winter promises

Tomatoes rosy as perfect babies' buttocks,
eggplants glossy as waxed fenders,
purple neon flawless glistening
peppers, pole beans fecund and fast
growing as Jack's Viagra-sped stalk,
big as truck tire zinnias that mildew
will never wilt, roses weighing down
a bush never touched by black spot,
brave little fruit trees shouldering up
their spotless ornaments of glass fruit:

I lie on the couch under a blanket
of seed catalogs ordering far
too much. Sleet slides down
the windows, a wind edged
with ice knifes through every crack.
Lie to me, sweet garden-mongers:
I want to believe every promise,
to trust in five pound tomatoes
and dahlias brighter than the sun
that was eaten by frost last week.

Where beach umbrellas spread gaudy circles

Walking by the ocean on a winter
day, we find the beach narrowed,
chewed by storm, the cliffs
gouged and crumbling

green veins of clay exposed.
Snow on sand, like icing
on pound cake. Sea ducks
bob on the iron waves.

A seal is hauled up, weary.
We feel the heat escaping
our bodies, rising like white
smoke, dissipating. Cold

encloses us like a glove.
The wind scrapes our faces
till we turn and trot back,
cold crawling into our sleeves—

a snake we'll bring home.
We will never be warm again,
we say, piling into the truck
which starts reluctantly, coughing.

Winter occupies the beach
entrenched with its barbed wire
emplacements of ice and wind.
We are not welcome. We flee.

Take it as it comes

I watch through the high window
a mating dance of hawks over the unfledged maple:
red shouldered hawks turning about
each other in the aluminum sky,
transfixed by the other, desire
forming the core of their tightening spiral.

Spring comes slowly from the ground up,
seeping first into the grass that rises
over its dead forebears, bed of light straw,
pushing up in the spears of the bulbs
that hold the future within, that will
flower in scarlet, in egg yolk, in sky.

Spring uncoils in the bushes, lilac,
honeysuckle, while the oaks stand
barren as bedposts. But the willow,
the willow by the shallow silver
brook furling over stones is bright
chartreuse with sap and light.

Spring comes early to the skunks,
to the chickadees calling, to the geese—
arrowheads thrusting north—to the river

spilling its banks drowning meadows
and to the willow that leans, feet
happily wet, letting its hair hang down.

In the light of the spring moon
you show not yellow green but
silver mermaid hair, and the moon
you lean toward is the face scattered
shattered on the brook raging now
and singing loudly all night.

The gardener's litany

We plant, it is true.
I start the tiny seedlings
in peat pots, water, feed.

But the garden is alive
in the night with its own
adventures. Slugs steal

out, snails carry their
spiraled houses upward,
rabbits hop over the fence.

The garden like a green
and bronze goddess loves
zucchini this year but will

not give us cucumbers.
She does as she pleases.
Purple beans but no yellows.

Serve me, she whispers,
maybe I will give you tomatoes,
or maybe I will hatch into

thousands of green caterpillars.
Maybe I will grow only bindweed,

joe-pye weed and dandelions.

All gardeners worship weather
and luck. We begin in compost
and end in decay. The life

of one is the death of the other.
Beetles eat squash plant. Bird
eats beetle. Soil eats all.

Eclipse at the solstice

New moon and the hottest sun:
It should be the day of the triumphant
sun marching like a red elephant
up the lapis arch of sky.

The moon is invisible, shy,
almost wounded. She draws
the thin short darkness around her
like a torn dress.

Then in the fat of the afternoon
she slides over the sun
enveloping him. I have
conquered, she croons,

brought darkness and put the birds
to sleep, raised the twilight wind.
But then his corona shines
around her and she sees.

You really are a lion with mane
of white fire, you beauty. So
she gives him the day back,
slowly, and lets him roar.

A kind of theft

It is the season of making vinegars,
tarragon, rosemary-orange, purple
basil, dill, chive blossom, cilantro:
aromatic, stoppered into bottles.

I take great handfuls and handfuls
of herbs, spendthrift, greedy,
and bruise them in a mortar.
I punish them for being.

Then I heat the various bought
vinegars, the cider, the wine,
the rice, the plain and nasty,
and pour them over the beaten herbs.

The sour preserves them. The harsh
liquid surrounds and leaches
from the green stuff its ghostly
essence. For three weeks

I shake and turn. Then
I filter and discard the herbs,
throw out what was so fresh.
I have extracted its soul.

I have turned it to garbage.
How often I do the same
to parts of myself, to adventures
and mishaps and terrors,

to the deaths of those dear,
to the pleasures of sleek
and sliding flesh, all the leaves
and flowers of my passing days.

The rain as wine

It is a ripe rain
coming down in big fat drops
like grapes dropping on the roof—
white grapes round as moons.

It is coming in waves
whooshing through the trees.
Silvery, intimate, it softens
and washes the parched air.

It falls on my face
like a blessing.
It sweetens my body
rolling down my upstretched arms.

The rain blesses us
as it opens the cracked earth
as it opens us to itself:
the sweet gush of August rain.

The corner

It's turning. A sharp corner of blue falence.
Oh, I know it will get hot again.
The roof will smell burnt outside my window.

The leaves will loll, limp as old clothes
washed too many times, faded
into a dull sullen dollar bill green.

But the red will start with the Virginia
creeper strangling the locust in crimson.
The poison ivy will glow like roses.

The wind is heftier and carries a knife.
Night comes perceptibly sooner
and hangs around, still pressing

its muzzle against the windows
when we wake. Its breath
like a warning strokes the back of my neck.

All creatures now move faster
except the cricket, whose chirp loosens
as the temperature drops.

Summer like an old lion lies down
in the tawny weeds under the oak.
The swallows are lined up on wires

gossiping about their summer like the folks
returning to the city, who don't imagine
how we stand straighter now and smile

at each other as if we had just been
wakened to the land brightening
while the sun it swallowed now spills out.

Taconic at midnight

At eleven we headed home, north
on the Taconic Parkway to the Mass Pike,
a mild late September night with fog
drifting in great hanks like white Spanish
moss, wavering in translucent
banners across the narrow highway,
diffusing moonlight, deflecting our beams.

Almost at once we began to see them:
deer congregated on each side where
the woods opened, dozens in a clearing,
bucks in the road, does milling about.
We drove slower and slower, inching
past, steering among them who ignored
our intrusion. They were intent

on each other, for this gathering
was a mating mart, like a mixer:
but they were serious, examining
each other with desperate attention,
an air of silky sexy tension roiling
like the fog that sank and lifted
bedazzling their sleek flanks,

their shaking antlers. The road
did not belong. It should have been
rolled up like a bale of wire and stowed,
for this was a night of the ancient gods
when America floated on the turtle's back
and all things were still pristine
as the lucent brown eye of a virgin doe.

The equinox rush

The swan heads south in the night sky.
Overhead, the sharp white triangle
of Altair, Deneb and Vega prickles.

At dawn there is a hint of frost,
only etched on the truck down
at the foot of the drive.

A sharp shinned hawk eyes
chickadees at the feeder, swoops.
That afternoon over High Head

I see two more hawks passing
missile lean, hurrying before
a wind I cannot feel.

Everything quickens. Squirrels
rush to feed. Monarchs among
the milkweed raggedly zigzag

toward South America. Too early
for the final harvest, too early
to mulch and protect, too soon

to take off the screens, still

some sharp corner has been turned.
I am stirred to finish something.

A hint of cold frames the day
and compresses it. Urgency
is the drug of the moment.

Find a task and do it, the red
of the Virginia creeper warns.
The sunset is a brushfire.

I am hurrying, I am running hard
toward I don't know what,
but I mean to arrive before dark.

After the loss

A storm rips the leaves
from wet black branches
twisting like wrought iron.
The ground is yellow, crimson.

The sky is heavy as lead
but light seeps upward.
Hope from an unexpected
quarter, that the wind will

quiet its squalling and sleep,
that at last we will be freed
from the battered cowering
shell of house, its shingles

dark with water. Sun
is a memory of something
cherished, lost. Hope
is hard sometimes in the

late days of the year,
a life, so that we grasp
hard for it even in the
litter of dead leaves.

The aria

One crow comes now every morning
to scout the compost heap. Have
we put out anything good?

She—I cannot sex crows so it's
free choice—has begun to visit
the pine near the window

where she watches me on the treadmill.
If I open the window and address her,
she answers. I think I amuse her.

We eat most of our leftovers, but
now and then there is old catfood,
something spoiled, a moldy

stew forgotten in the refrigerator's
hinterland. Then she calls, calls
and her mates come flapping.

Just before Pesach, there's a feast
of crackers, breakfast cereals,
croutons. They throw a party.

The other afternoon she began
to sing. At first I could not imagine
what I was hearing, but she knows me

and did not stop when I slowly
approached. It was contralto, slow,
a complete aria of molten longing

addressed perhaps to the compost
pile, perhaps to me, perhaps
to a missing lover or dead chick.

I can't guess, but the crow looked
at me and I looked back at her
and I bowed my head as she sang.

Leonids over us

The sky is streaked with them
burning holes in black space—
like fireworks, someone says
all friendly in the dark chill
of Newcomb Hollow in November,
friends known only by voices.

We lie on the cold sand and it
embraces us, this beach
where locals never go in summer
and boast of their absence. Now
we lie eyes open to the flowers
of white ice that blaze over us

and seem to imprint directly
on our brains. I feel the earth,
rolling beneath as we face out
into the endlessness we usually
ignore. Past the evanescent
meteors, infinity pulls hard.

Little Lights

Little lights

Tonight I light the first candle
on the chanukiyah by the window
and then a second in the bathtub,
the yahrzeit candle for your death.

I am always sad the first night
of a holiday when we should rejoice.
This night nineteen years ago
the light of your mind snuffed out.

The Chanukah candles burn quickly
two hours and they gutter out
their short time burnt up.
We did not know how old you were—

you'd always fudged your age,
you had no birth certificate—
I don't know if you knew
your birth date and place, for real.

Grandma always gave a different
answer and then shrugged. Your
mother is younger than me and
older than you, what else matters?

Yes, there's Moses and David,
Babylon and the Talmud,
Maimonides, and then we appear
out of a cloud of smoke and haze

of old blood there among the Jew-
haters clutching a few bundles.
My people poor, without names,
histories vanished into the hard soil

but we had stories with pedigrees:
my female ancestors told them,
Lilith, the Golem, Rabbi Nachman,
the Maccabees, all simultaneous

all swarming around my bed
all caught in my hair as you
washed it with tar soap, relating
fables, family gossip, bubele

maisehs, precious handed down
the true family jewels, my dowry.
Those little flames you lit in my
mind burn on paper for you,

your true yahrzeit, all year
every year of my aging life.

Seder with comet

The comet was still hanging in the sky
that year at Pesach, and of course
the full moon, as every year.

After the bulk of the seder, after
the long rich redolent meal, we all
went out on the road walking away

from the house whose lights we had
dimmed. There on the velvet playing
field of night we saw the moon rolling

toward us like a limestone millwheel
the whole sky pouring to fill our heads
a little drunk with the sweet wine

so that the stars sank in with a whisper
like a havdalah candle doused in wine
giving a little electric buzz to the brain.

Then we saw it, the comet like the mane
of a white lion, something holy to mark
this one more Passover with all of us

together, my old commune mates, friends
from here and the city, children I have known
since birth, all standing with our faces turned

up like pale sunflowers to the icy fire.
Then we went back to the house, drank
the last cup and sang till we were hoarse.

Quieting by the bay

Sitting on the cold cement steps
at the dike watching cormorants
dive, black sleek onyx
midnight sheen on their feathers,
I came to meditate but watch
instead, and it works.

I am diving in the cold waters
of the bay, light tickling
above me and alewives
slipping silvery below.
I am rising now on sharp
wings into the low November

sun, burnt umber across
the pale dune where a ruddy
fox crosses among bleached
grass making wind circles.
I partake, mind thinning
its soap bubble to the horizon.

Sometimes while I am chanting

Sometimes while I am chanting
the Hebrew words become liquid
as warm rain and I slip through
them as if they were water parting
to let me down to a clear place.

Sometimes when I am praying
the words stop and the darkness
rises like water in a basin
and I come into silence
rich as the heart of a rose.

Sometimes when I meditate
light swells along my limbs
and opens sweet as apple
blossoms from the hard wood
of my knobbly spine.

Light slides behind my eyes
light rises in my throat
light pulses in my chest.
There is no I only you only
light burning and unburnt.

Time of year

A time of year of dusty ritual
and fresh apples and pumpkins.
To believe is to work at believing.
They say that labor is prayer, and prayer
is certainly work.

Dust on my forehead, dust
in my eyes, burning dust.
Indifference is worse than despair
because despair still cares.
Dust stifles any cry. Yet

I go at dawn to sit on the dike
meditating on the horizon's rim
two cormorants sentineled
on a dingy waiting for alewives
different hungers but fierce

both of us, me apparently still
but cooking within. Then wings
spread wide in my chest,
the great beak strikes me
till I break into light.

Illumination never lasts, but it
comes, it comes, and all I can
do is prepare, to open, to
wait like the hungry cormorant
for the first flicker of light.

Sins of omission

Little gravestones like mushrooms
sprung up with the moist dawn:
little gravestones like buttons
I constantly open and close
to let the dead out into my eyes.

My watch tells me it is time
to remember, my watch tells
me I will always forget.
Some faces come back only
in the heavy sack of the night.

Some names are recited
only in dreams and when
the alarm saws into me
they are gone like moths
that flutter off if you wave

your hand. I will never
forget I promise, then wind
stirs the ghosts into nothing.
Memory fades, an old rug
worked perhaps into a tree

of life, perhaps a garden.
What was bright red now
is stained like rust. Only
in the knotted prayer of a poem
can I make those colors gleam.

Shadows on darkness

A yahrzeit candle
in its glass shell
stands in the bathtub
the flame shivering
beating like a heart.

The shimmering
spiral of fire
throws latticed shadows
—design of the glass—
on the longest night.

Your death accompanies
me to bed,
your face flickering.
In the dead of winter
your life guttered out.

My life is more than
half past. Midnight
is only a halfway
house on the solstice
dark. Love for

the dead is a candle
in a mirror,
the flame agile
but cold, and darkness
gathering like a storm.

Tapuz: an orange

When women were beginning to be ordained as rabbis, Susannah Heschel was speaking at a synagogue in Florida. A man rose in anger. "A woman belongs on the bimah as much as an orange belongs on the seder plate!"

Round you are and bright as a newly risen moon.
You are sweet and acid, dessert and medicine.
You carry within your curves the future
of your kind, those pale seeds winking
from the sections, each an embryo tree.

Come into your own and shine,
where the only roundness was the almost
hidden plate bearing up the ritual items.
Be subject as well as object. Sing
in your orangeness of female strength.

Clash if you need to. Roll if you must.
Center the plate about your glow.
We are, we will be, we become: rabbis,
yes, cantors, shapers, prophets, creating
a new Judaism that is yours and ours.

The cameo

My only time in Naples
the day we went to Pompeii
street sellers had them: big fine cameos
just like the one my grandma
left to me, a brooch. Seeing them

was finding a footprint in the street:
her small feet like my mother's
had passed here with her great
sophisticated love. Her rabbi
father married them on his deathbed.

They left Russia under a load of straw
a price on his head, no papers.
In Naples he sold his gold
watch to buy them passports
taking the name Bunin, after

the writer he admired.
What will you do in America
the anarchist seller asked.
Make a revolution, he declaimed.
So he got a good price.

Off to Ellis Island, where the
immigration inspector added
an extra *n* and let them slip

in, Grandma secretly pregnant
under her too big black dress.

She insisted on mourning her father
though her husband objected.
But she kept her long chestnut
hair against custom, to please
him, who said such glory should

never be sacrificed, and any angels
tempted would have to come through
him. She did not know yet
he would be unfaithful, give her
eleven children to raise in squalor,

make no revolution but organize
unions, be killed by Pinkertons.
In Naples she danced through exotic
dangerous streets on his arm, proud
he could speak Italian and bargain

not only for passports cheap
but carved head and shoulders of a fine
looking woman he said resembled
her, and she was pleased although
already she did not believe him.

Miriam's cup

This cup of fresh water suggests Miriam's well, which accompanied the children of Israel through the desert. In Miriam's cup of water, we have a parallel to Elijah's cup of wine. Elijah's stands for redemption to come; Miriam's concerns the redemption occurring daily in our lives.

The cup of Elijah holds wine;
the cup of Miriam holds water.
Wine is more precious
until you have no water.

Water that flows in our veins,
water that is the stuff of life
for we are made of breath
and water, vision

and fact. Elijah is
the extraordinary; Miriam
brings the daily wonders:
the joy of a fresh morning

like a newly prepared table,
a white linen cloth on which
nothing has yet spilled.
The descent into the heavy

waters of sleep healing us.
The scent of baking bread,
roasted chicken, fresh herbs,
the faces of friends across

the table. What sustains us
every morning, every evening,
the common miracles
like the taste of cool water.

Colors Passing Through Us

Colors passing through us

Purple as tulips in May, mauve
into lush velvet, purple
as the stain blackberries leave
on the lips, on the hands,
the purple of ripe grapes
sunlit and warm as flesh.

Every day I will give you a color,
like a new flower in a bud vase
on your desk. Every day
I will paint you, as women
color each other with henna
on hands and on feet.

Red as henna, as cinnamon,
as coals after the fire is banked,
the cardinal in the feeder,
the roses tumbling on the arbor
their weight bending the wood
the red of the syrup I make from petals.

Orange as the perfumed fruit
hanging their globes on the glossy tree,
orange as pumpkins in the field,
orange as butterflyweed and the monarchs

who come to eat it, orange as my
cat running lithe through the high grass.

Yellow as a goat's wise and wicked eyes,
yellow as a hill of daffodils,
yellow as dandelions by the highway,
yellow as butter and egg yolks,
yellow as a school bus stopping you,
yellow as a slicker in a downpour.

Here is my bouquet, here is a sing
song of all the things you make
me think of, here is oblique
praise for the height and depth
of you and the width too.
Here is my box of new crayons at your feet.

Green as mint jelly, green
as a frog on a lily pad twanging,
the green of cos lettuce upright
about to bolt into opulent towers,
green as Grande-Chartreuse in a clear
glass, green as wine bottles.

Blue as cornflowers, delphiniums,
bachelor's buttons. Blue as Roquefort,

blue as Saga. Blue as still water.
Blue as the eyes of a Siamese cat.
Blue as shadows on new snow, as a spring
azure sipping from a puddle on the blacktop.

Cobalt as the midnight sky
when day has gone without a trace
and we lie in each other's arms
eyes shut and fingers open
and all the colors of the world
pass through our bodies like strings of fire.

The grammatical difference between *lay* and *lie*

The first takes an object: takes
its objective. The second is complete
enclosed, onanistic. It rests
in itself like a stone.

I love the moment when the blossoms
drop and the ground is carpeted
thick in fallen petals.
This—I think as I lie under the foamy cherry,
under the arch of the red, red roses
dripping from their trellis—
is what I would really call
a flower bed
where you lay me sweetly
and all my buds burst open.

Love's clay

Love is a lumpy thing.
Infatuation is peacock tales,
fountains of rose petals,
always music underneath
like a movie crescendoing.

Love is cutting onions
for supper when you are
already tired. Love is patched
of hope and habit and desire,
a tent mended nightly.

Love is tough as a bone
you gnaw on, suck out
the marrow. Love is a bone
of which you make soup
and, surprise, it sustains you.

Infatuation is fun, a tango
in a grove of mirrors. Love
is just work, what you do
one day after the next
like bricks laid end to end

and finally infatuation
leaves you with a sticky
sweet residue in the bottom
of the glass, and love is all
you remember as you're dying.

Old moon cradling the new moon

What we have known is fully formed
but fading, a chord no longer quite
audible but resonating in the bones.

What we will be together is just a sliver
of light, a whisper, a tone too high
to hear yet but alerting the nerves.

What we have been contains
what we will be, although it is new
as first milk from a swollen breast.

What we desire rides the night
like a storm of tiny feathers, blossoms
of ice and pinpricks of fire.

Where we will go is rooted in where
we have been, in each other's arms
as if twinned in the womb, and now

the womb opens on a new beast
an elegant hybrid of cat and eagle,
a flower fully armed and fragrant

with the essences of could be, might
be, want to be, with the promise of birth
under the sign of the skinniest moon.

Chilled through

Waking in the morning without you,
you sleeping two thousand miles
west where it is earlier and dark still

I am silly and sad and don't get up.
The day seems spoiled milk already.
The day is too thin to walk on.

It will give way beneath me.
I look forward to nothing
but its shriveling with twilight

another empty jar of night
two more bleak awakenings
until you return like summer

in February, my own miracle.
This lack whines in me, a wind
off the salt flats. The taste

of an empty glass. Wanting exhausts me.
I wish I could hibernate like a bear
and not even dream till you come.

The first time I tasted you

The first time I tasted you I thought
strange: metallic, musty, with salt
and cinnamon, the sea
and the kitchen
safety and danger.

The second time I tasted you I thought
known: already known,
perhaps in an oasis of dream
in the desert of a hard night
the dry wind parching me.

I tasted the fruit of a tree
that promised not life
but love, the knowledge
of being known at last
down to my gnarly pit.

What we know and don't
of each other goes on
a voyage not infinite
but long enough, notching
years on our bones.

From your body I eat
and drink all I will ever
know of passionate love
from now till death
drains the chalice.

Black leaves

The forest of hair
we are lost in it.
Buried in our embrace
we find each other
and wriggle into burrows
through sweet moist earth.

Our eyes are closed:
blind as silky moles
whose senses taste
the darkness
like the bouquet
of fine wine.

In the kingdom of touch
flesh blossoms:
black peonies.
Not the eyes, not the brain
but the entire body
knows and loves

enters and is
entered wholly.
Marry me again
in the tangled briar
of knotted limbs, the dark
wilderness of desire.

The animal kingdom

In bed our bodies mutate.
We have many small supple bones
so we can coil round each other
warm blooded serpents slithering
twisting, skin dancing on skin.

In bed our bodies change.
Wings poke through our shoulder
blades and open umbrellalike
and then we beat up to the ceiling,
we rise through the roof,

we soar into obsidian night
then dive clutched like falcons,
talons interlocked, the wind
beating in our hot blood
as we shriek our razor sharp joy.

In bed we are small and cosy,
mice in a nest of feathers.
We purr like kittens tumbling
over each other's furry flanks
and nipping with sharp teeth.

In bed we act the grace
of dolphins arcing like a wheel,
the grace of water falling
from a cliff white and sparkling
in a roar of spume.

In a moment we will be our
mundane selves flopping in a net
of unpaid bills and Things that Must
be Done, and aren't, email,
grocery lists and fungoid nails.

But now we are stately giraffes
nibbling the high browse of fore
heads; tigers stalking our sweet
prey through pubic jungles; lords
of the animal kingdom of sex.

How it goes with us

Love is the secret lining of the day.
Love is the taste of cappuccino in bed
in the mornings while the cats walk
round us and light streams in the east
windows across the marsh where night herons
nest, and through the tall stark pines.

Love is the inner meaning of the word:
I'll talk to you, I'll call you.
Should I come home at four?
Appointments of flesh to flesh,
rhythms rising under the blather,
stress and computer blur of work.

Love is the satin lining of the dark,
the night rising over us, wet
and salty and heavy as a body stretched
upon ours, our selves that merge
in the center and on the edges, flowing
into the other like black serpent rivers.

Love is the word underlying silence.
Love is the secret tether stretching
between us, gossamer steel.
Love is the road we walk on toward death
and as we climb its hardscrabble rocks
our hands are invisibly joined.

Black taffeta

The night is darkest maroon tonight
like a black tulip. No moon unzips
the charcoal fleece of clouds.

Yet someone is prancing in the dry
leaves under the rhododendrons,
a child of night plays there like a puppy.

Under the bleached pine needles
little life seethes and ceases.
Moths hurl themselves against the screen

like autistic babies banging their heads.
One spreads out his tiger stripes.
One is green as lime gelatin.

We are the light they thrust toward.
In the bed we rock and pitch
striking tiger eyes of sparks.

Then a dark blaze of passion sleek
as a panther's flank. As we collapse, an owl
calls again, again, like a clock striking.

Firebird

Washed in light, laved in its glitter
and rush, we turn and turn again
our eyes full of each other.

We burn without ash, bees
wax candles loosing perfume
of delight but staying whole.

We come together into a bloom
too bright to see, sun-flower
with petals of fire, corona

invisible except in the dark of
eclipse. We are each other's
miracle, the spine alight

the brain a quieting coal
the flesh become liquid fire
silky as phoenix feathers.

Worlds without end

Whenever you touch my mind unexpectedly
as a furry tail brushing my cheek;
whenever you surprise me with a word
that rises like a walking stick from a twig
and lumbers off on six legs leaving
me staring because I saw only bark;
whenever you appear with daisies or roses,
with oysters or corn or a secret book
I imagined having, gifts dropped
in my lap like fresh picked apples;
whenever you turn small calamities
into jokes sharp as onions in my nose;
whenever you swing suddenly and drop
words of praise over me like scented veils;
whenever I taste your uniqueness
like a splash of lemon juice on my tongue;
I know I know I will never be done
knowing you on and on; and always
as I proceed there is more of you to know.

Rising in Perilous Hope

Rising in perilous hope

What can I hold in my hands this morning
that will not flow through my fingers?

What words can I say that will catch
in your mind like burrs, chiggers that burrow?

If my touch could heal, I would lay my hands
on your bent head and bellow prayers.

If my words could change the weather
or the government or the way the world

twists and guts us, fast or slow,
what could I do but what I do now?

I fit words together and say them;
it is a given like the color of my eyes.

I hope it makes a small difference, as
I hope the drought will break and the morning

come rising out of the ocean wearing
a cloak of clean sweet mist and swirling terns.

Burnishing memory

I am learning how to remember
little colored crayon nubs of my childhood,
the sun coming through mason jars
of peaches still scalding from the canner,
the fat chalk the brakemen would throw
when we begged, perfect
for scrawling dirty words on sidewalks.

I save the newly found pieces of memory
like bright exotic stamps carefully put in
to the scrapbooks of a collection.
Unlike butterflies, collecting them
does not kill them, but captured,
saved, they become vibrant.
Soon they grow bigger.

I am building a simulacrum of my life
as untrue as maps. I remember when
I learned those red arteries and blue
veins of roads were just cement
or asphalt, not the scarlet road
I had imagined our car roaring over,
like the first time I heard "silk road."

So I am neglecting the vast hangers
full of nothing, the tunnels of boredom,
the days leaked out in classrooms
of despair, the banality of dusting.
Instead I build a tower of beautiful

junk, the blue sapphire glass of terror,
the winking red stars of sex, the purple

suns of transcendence, the white
light of insight flashing, the intricate
webs of belief and refusal, the homely
satisfying bricks of friendship, books
and recipes and yes, maps of places
I dreamed into being and inhabited
a season, a lifetime, a glimmering moment.

The new era, c. 1946

It was right after the war of my childhood
World War II, and the parks were wide open.
The lights were all turned on, house
lights, street lights, neon like green
and purple blood pumping the city's heart.
I had grown up in brown out, black out,
my father the air raid warden going
house to house to check that no pencil
of light stabbed out between blackout curtains.
Now it was summer and Detroit was celebrating.

Fireworks burst open their incandescent petals
flaring in arcs down into my wide eyes.
A band was playing "Stars and Stripes Forever."
Then the lights came on brighter and starker
than day and sprayers began to mist the field.
It was the new miracle DDT in which we danced
its faint perfumy smell like privet along the sidewalks.
It was comfort in mist, for there would be no more
mosquitoes forever, and now we would always be safe.

Out in Nevada soldiers were bathing in fallout.
People downwind of the tests were drinking
heavy water out of their faucets. Cancer
was the rising sign in the neon painted night.
Little birds fell out of the trees but no one
noticed. We had so many birds then.
In Europe American cigarettes were money.
Here all the kids smoked on street corners.
I used to light kitchen matches with my thumbnail.

My parents threw out their Depression ware
and bought Melmac plastic dishes.
They believed in plastic and the promise
that when they got old, they would go
to Florida and live like the middle class.
My brother settled in California with a new
wife and his old discontent. New car,
new refrigerator, Mama and Daddy have new hats.
Crouch and cover. Ashes, all fall down.

The yellow light

When I see—obsolete, forgotten—
a yellow porchlight, I am transported
to muggy Michigan evenings.
My breath is thick with July.

We are playing pinochle.
Every face card is a relative.
Now we are playing Hearts
but I am the Queen of Spades.

Mosquitoes hum over the weedy
lake. An owl groans in the pines.
Moths hurl themselves against
the screens, a dry brown rain.

Yellow makes every card black.
The eyes of my uncles are avid.
They are playing for pennies
and blood. One shows off

a new Buick, one a new wife.
The women are whispering
about bellies and beds.
It always smells like fried perch.

I am afraid I will never grow up.
I think the owl is calling me
over the black water to hide
in the pines and turn, turn

into something strange and dark
with wings and talons and words
of a more powerful language
than uncles and aunts know,
than uncles and aunts understand.

Frozen as far as the eye can see

A white pond: icefishing in Michigan.
I was twelve and bored.
My father and I sat in a little
hut—I liked that part—

staring at a hole and black
water, staring at a bobber
waiting for a fish I didn't want
except for something to happen.

Shivering in the dark in the middle
of the lake frozen to a nondescript
white field, I longed for demons
and corpses, anything at all.

My adolescence stretched out
beyond the horizon, pallid,
featureless, and any tracks crossing
were going noplace I wanted to be.

Flying over the Nebraska of my life

So much of our lives dissolves.
What did I do the day before
I met you? You remember
what I was wearing that holiday.
What did I wear the next morning?
What did I write the day my mother died?

I fly at night over the plains.
There is a cluster of lights,
a starfish shape glittering. Then
darkness and darkness.
Then another clump bearing
long daisy petals of roadway.

Then nothing again. How much
of my living has fled like water
into sand. The sand is not
even damp to the hand.
Tears and wine and sparkling
water all vanish the same.

I know looking out the plane's
dirty window that there are houses,
barns, roads, trees, stores
distinct in that darkness I once

drove through. I knew them and will
never know them again.

The plane is flying from lighted
place to lighted place, but
our arc is from the dark into
brightness then back into darkness.
I want to possess my own life like a
necklace, pearl by pearl of light.

Roomers, rumors

My mother took in roomers. Salesmen mostly.
I wrote my poems on their invoices,
their expense reports, pink and green.

Once a week we changed their beds.
Washed the smelly towels. Cleaned.
Rummaged their things, prying.

I have a right to know, Mother said.
I didn't think so, but I was curious.
Their lives were just expense reports.

Smells of unwashed socks and aftershave.
Photo of a child visited five years ago.
Girlie magazines, detective fiction,

maps of where they had to go.
Mother always knew where they had been.
His wife left him for a butcher. He caught

his girlfriend in bed with his brother.
He did time for bad checks in Wisconsin.
He was drinking and ran off the road.

The only roomer I ever befriended was three
years older than me and pregnant,

up to Detroit for her husband's job at Fords.

I held her when she miscarried.
Her blood soaked my blouse.
Her screams made furrows in my brain.

No more women, Mother said. *Men
are easier.* I slid past them in the hall.
I made myself invisible and kept silent.

By this time I was a roomer myself
in my parents' house, spinning lies
around myself, a cocoon inside which

I altered beyond their guessing. I hid
my poems from her, slipped my journal
into the wall and went on the road

selling my dreams to anyone, to you.

Borrowed lives

In the Detroit neighborhood
where I grew up, reputations
were knitted and tattered,
stories circulated quick
as numbers runners' circuits.
We smoked each other's secrets.

In the first place that I lived
with my second husband, Cambridge
a mile from Harvard, neighbors
nodded and dismissed you.
They were reluctant to part
with their names, like passwords.

Yet evenings I would slip along
those polite brick-sidewalked
streets and nobody lowered
shades. I stole their lives
to play with, assigning vices,
virtues, pasts, trysts, dramas.

One couple was always standing
her shoulder sharply raised,
his arms folded making a fort.
A white cat sat on a cushion watching

through a bay window. A kid
threw a violin across his room.

I saw lovers kiss and strike each
other, I studied pictures on walls,
walls of books, chandeliers—
drawing dubious inferences.
A couple ate waving their forks.
A man lay on a couch singing.

Lonely, held in a stiff new
marriage like linen not yet washed
soft, I spied with baffled tenderness,
curiosity rank as old onions,
on these glimpses, making them
people the dollhouse of my life.

Mexico City, 1968, summer

We were lovers there in that alley
of rain that came down heavy
as blood and blood that spurted
splashing against the old walls
like the monsoon rain.

We were lovers briefly in the fog
of terror, when it was not clear
who moved toward us and who
fled abandoning us, who sought
our death and who ignored it.

The partially dissected bodies
of student leaders lay neatly
arranged on grounds of the univers-
ity each morning, if a person
with entrails spiraled out

can be called tidy. When I
screamed it was in my own
language and I fell into you
seeking comfort as if you were
a door I could close and lock.

Photo instead of friend

A friend took that photograph.
He had come to Provincetown:
a married lover met him in secret
an affair trickled over a decade.

He died the way so many did
and do, slowly as water
evaporating and then all gone
the wasting pain finally over.

Missing goes on, sometimes
louder, sometimes inaudible
but there is always a place calling.
Wasn't there a door in that wall?

Didn't an apple tree bloom
in that window? I recall when
the peacock glazed vase broke.
I remember rabbity hills of blowing

grass, now subdivisions. And him
warm behind the camera, clucking,
offering encouragement, compliments:
candy bribes to a child to smile.

I mosey along managing to ignore
places we shared till something pricks
through the callus. How bright then
the spurt of memory and blood.

Dignity

Near the end of your life you regard
me with a gaze clear and lucid
saying simply, I am, I will not be.

How foolish to imagine animals
don't comprehend death. Old
cats study it like a recalcitrant mouse.

You seek out warmth for your bones
close now to the sleek coat
that barely wraps them,

little knobs of spine, the jut
of hip bones, the skull
my fingers lightly caress.

Sometimes in the night you cry:
a deep piteous banner of gone
desire and current sorrow,

the fear that the night is long
and hungry and you pace
among its teeth feeling time

slipping through you cold and
slick. If I rise and fetch you back
to bed, you curl against me purring

able to grasp pleasure by the nape
even inside pain. Your austere
dying opens its rose of ash.

The garden of almost

The sun fits over the black top
of my head, a toasting helmet.
The leaves of the sugar maple
are opening their wide hands
pawing at the south wind.

Although the jackals of war
are feeding on riven flesh,
although the wind that smells
of clean salt bears exhaust,
deadly particles that silt the lungs—

in the moment all roundness
swells with fecundity, seeds
in the rich earth, buds opening,
fruit small and fuzzy beading
on the peach bough, peony

showing a red slit of silk. My
cheek painted with fertile black
mud, I lie on my side in the row
between broccoli and spinach,
a ladybug climbing my hot arm

and I hear only birdsong,
finch, cardinal, distant gull,
oriole among tiny cherries.
I am whole, here as a robin.
Momentarily I love the world.

On the water, reflecting herself

The swan, the wide throbbing wings
that lift her up, the outstretched neck
that coils to an S on the waters:
how bright she is in the dawn flashing.

In the night sky she is overhead
her bright stars bluish and white.
In fall she leaves us. What south
then does she travel toward?

Ivory bird of day, silently
you cross the pond as if sailing
intent, avid. Like your cousin
the moon, you have your cycles,

you come and go, you wander far
and return, and whenever we see you
our mouths form the O of surprise
for your gleaming, for your dangerous beak.

I awake feathered

I awake covered in feathers.
Iridescent, I gleam
in the milky dawn.

I shimmer like a rainbow
hanging in the air.
I raise my arm over my head

and the wing extends.
This morning I will take
flight, take and use it.

Later perhaps I will molt,
dwindle into human
again, but my power

fills me now like music
loud and surging. I rise
over the house, the gardens.

I beat high into the crisp
limpid air, then float,
a kite no string controls.

It can't last, but it shouldn't.
Pinnacles are of the moment.
Right now I belong up here.

The joys of a bad reputation

The rumor that my poems are written
by a brigade of Burmese cats typing randomly
on special computers is purr propaganda.

Before we went out, my husband was solemnly
told by a Cambridge therapist I had never
met that I lived with three men.

Every night I had them strip
naked and parade before me.
I would point to one and say, *Him.*

He considered this a likely
exaggeration. To his skepticism
I owe my marriage.

I meet people who believe I'm rich.
Apparently my poems have sold to the movies.
My novels are on all the tabloid shows.

Some believe upon meeting a male professor
I drop to one knee and bite his balls.
Then I summon my cortege of mad amazon

shock troops. We behead
all the statues. We take off our clothes
and dance naked on deans' desks.

No, my cats do not write my novels.
They merely think up the ideas.
I do the actual typing myself.

In a previous existence
I was a perfect elephantine red rose
and gave Cotton Mather allergy attacks.

I plan to auction off rights to
manufacture my autobiography to the next
five interesting strangers I meet.

Are you interested? I am taking
sealed bribes. No outrageous
proffer will be refused.

Old cat crying

The old cat stands on the flagstone
path through the herb garden,
crying. She has what
the vet calls cognitive
dysfunction, as will we all
as will we all.

She is crying for the companion
who always came to her
from the time he drank
her milk, with whom she slept
four sharp ears from one
grey cushion of fur.

He should not have died
before her. She cries
for him to come. She
sniffed his body and knew
but she has forgotten
and he does not come.

I hold her and it is my
past I mourn, my mother,
lovers, friends whom
I shall never again summon
and the future's empty
silent rooms.

The lower crust

I make perfect pies, the dough light,
fragrant, faintly sweet as it crunches;
the filling is almost an afterthought.

I was taught by a woman I thought
loved me, but she wanted only the man
I lived with, bit into him and spit him out.

That friendship rotted from the inside,
a squash that looks perfect, smooth
skin, but when you cut into it, stinks,

a borer's home, brown and watery
the grub curled fat in the waste.
The perfect crust is all that remains

of a false smile, an easy lie, a promise
collapsed. Yet my pies give me more
pleasure than she ever could.

Traveling dream

I am packing to go to the airport
but somehow I am never packed.
I keep remembering more things
I keep forgetting.

Secretly the clock is bolting
forward ten minutes at a click
instead of one. Each time
I look away, it jumps.

Now I remember I have to find
the cats. I have four cats
even when I am asleep.
One is on the bed and I slip

her into the suitcase.
One is under the sofa. I
drag him out. But the tabby
in the suitcase has vanished.

Now my tickets have run away.
Maybe the cat has my tickets.
I can only find one cat.
My purse has gone into hiding.

Now it is time to get packed.
I take the suitcase down.
There is a cat in it but no clothes.
My tickets are floating in the bath

tub full of water. I dry them.
One cat is in my purse
but my wallet has dissolved.
The tickets are still dripping.

I look at the clock as it leaps
forward and see I have missed
my plane. My bed is gone now.
There is one cat the size of a sofa.

A conversation with memory

You are something I drag behind me
in the dust like a peacock's tail
sweeping up leaves, ignored
until something prompts that display:

then the dull weight of the forgotten
spreads out into a glorious fan
iridescent flightless feathers shining,
and the hundred eyes reporting.

Yes, memory, you are this weight
I lug about like an oversized briefcase,
like a too big too full suitcase
pulling my shoulder from its socket.

You are my shadow that weighs
more than lead. You turn on
in the night and your searchlight
vanishes the present and sleep.

I study how to make you more vivid,
stronger, and you suck me under
into viscous cold black waters
where my body too remembers,

opens lost gills and I breathe
your thick substance and you take

over my brain and instruct me
how to serve in the synagogue-

library-catacombs of your power.
Ah, you say, what could be weaker
than me, who resides in splinters,
in grandmother's tales, in fading

brown photographs, in evanescent
scents of tulip and black bean soup,
weak as a taper until you light
my flame with your mind.

Tasting evanescence

Eventually the sun darkens, sure.
Eventually the oceans boil dry
and the air thickens to smut.

But long before that, the silencing.
Paper crackles into confetti.
Ink fades. Discs become obsolete.

Poems in WordStar and MultiMate
corrode in junked computers.
Poems in Etruscan and Indo-European

in the lost languages of the lost tribes
of the California mountains, the male
and the female languages throats slit

bones burned, dust blowing
inscribe letters no one is left
to read, to say, to fix the air

into shapes of power or order.
Somewhere through the black matter
between the burning stars

poems are rushing toward us
in languages we cannot decipher
from planets dead as the moon.

All I can be sure of is this moment
of saying when the words rise
like champagne bubbles in my throat.

All I am sure of is this pellucid
moment when the words are no longer
inside me but we are in the words.

As the way narrows

We walked by a canal lined with linden
trees, rain pocking the surface
big drops spreading circles in circles.
We were staying at a pension in Toulouse
where the daughters went about all day
with their hair in pink curlers
like a fifties suburb, but the food
was straight from our dreams.

What did we expect of the years?
An easy path? Comfort handed
us like our morning café au lait
with a newspaper we did not bother
to translate and a perfect croissant?
Virtue rewarded with a nice pension?
Yet all day we were searching out
sites where resisters were tortured,

killed, where they fought their last
battles always outnumbered,
outgunned. Why should we be
surprised years later to find our teeth
pried from their sockets, our way
crooked over sharp red rocks
where rattlesnakes buzz their tails
and vultures idle above patiently.

I can remember hope, remember
ease, but as we age, the way
grows steeper. Yet we have
taken each other and hold hard.
In that unforgiving night we walk
now hand in hand alert as foxes
with our senses peeled raw
our steps still sure and bold.

ACKNOWLEDGMENTS

Various poems in this collection originally appeared in the following publications: *Buckle &, Calapooya, Calyx, Cape Cod Voice, Caprice, Chiron Review, Clay Palm Review, Coe Review, Connecticut Review, The Cortland Review, Earth's Daughters, An Earth Odyssey, Forward, Green Mountains Review, Jewish Women's Literary Annual, Joe, Kalliope, The Kenyon Review, The Louisiana Review, Lunar Calendar, Maine Times, Many Mountains Moving, The Massachusetts Review, The Montserrat Review, On the Issues, Orbis, The Paradoxes of Miriam, The Paterson Literary Review, Pif, Poetry International, Poiesis, Prairie Schooner, Princeton University Library Chronicle, River City, The Seattle Review, The Southern California Anthology, Tikkun, Tin House, Verve, Visions,* and *The Worcester Review.*

The following poems were previously published in *Sleeping with Cats, A Memoir* (Morrow/HarperCollins 2002): "Burnishing memory," "Dignity," "The good old days at home sweet home," "The new era c. 1946," and "Winter promises."

A NOTE ON THE TYPE

The text of this book was set in Minister, a typeface designed
by M. Fahrenwaldt for the German Schriftguss foundry in 1929.
A modern interpretation of the classic Venetian letter forms of
the fifteenth century, Minister is characterized by a calligraphic spirit,
well-defined concave shaped serifs, and broadly formed capital
letters.

Composed by NK Graphics, Keene, New Hampshire
Printed and bound by R. R. Donnelley, Harrisonburg, Virginia
Designed by Robert C. Olsson